Our Community Helpers

Doctors Help

by Dee Ready

Consulting editor: Gail Saunders-Smith, PhD

CAPSTONE PRESS
a capstone imprint

Pebble Books are published by Capstone Press,
1710 Roe Crest Drive, North Mankato, Minnesota 56003
www.capstonepub.com

Library of Congress Cataloging-in-Publication Data
Cataloging-in-Publication information is on file with the Library of Congress.
ISBN: 978-1-62065-078-3 (library binding)
ISBN: 978-1-62065-843-7 (paperback)
ISBN: 978-1-4765-1715-5 (ebook PDF)

Note to Parents and Teachers

The Our Community Helpers set supports national social studies
standards for how groups and institutions work to meet individual
needs. This book describes and illustrates doctors. The images
support early readers in understanding the text. The repetition of
words and phrases helps early readers learn new words. This book
also introduces early readers to subject-specific vocabulary words,
which are defined in the Glossary section. Early readers may need
assistance to read some words and to use the Table of Contents,
Glossary, Read More, Internet Sites, and Index sections of the book.

Printed in the United States of America in Stevens Point, Wisconsin.
092012   006937WZS13

Table of Contents

What Is a Doctor?

Doctors help sick or hurt people get better.
They also help healthy people stay healthy.

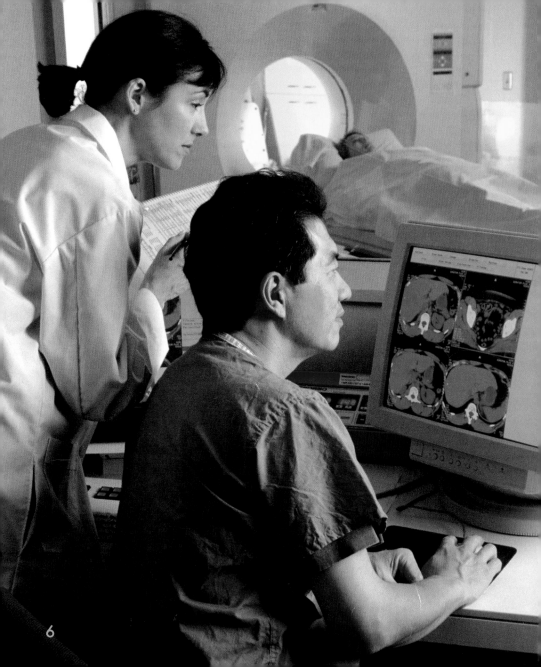

All doctors learn about
the human body.
But some doctors focus
on certain parts of the body.
Neurologists study the brain.

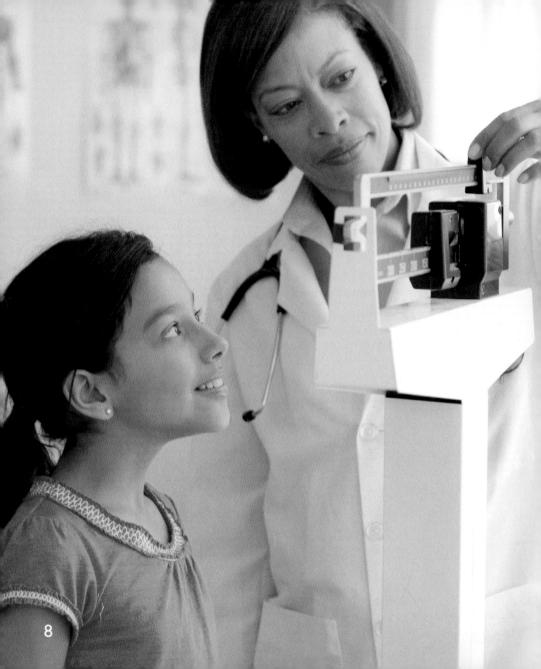

Other doctors care for certain kinds of patients. A doctor who sees only children is a pediatrician.

What Doctors Do

Doctors treat people
who are sick or hurt.

They give patients medicine.

They may set a broken bone.

Sometimes doctors do surgery.

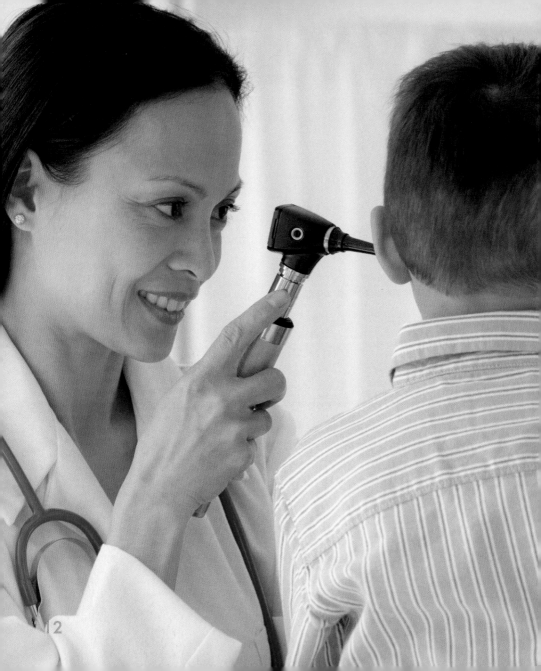

People also go to doctors for checkups. Doctors tell patients how to stay healthy. Doctors give shots to keep people from getting diseases.

Clothes and Tools

Doctors may wear white coats to see patients. They may also wear scrubs. Rubber gloves protect them from germs.

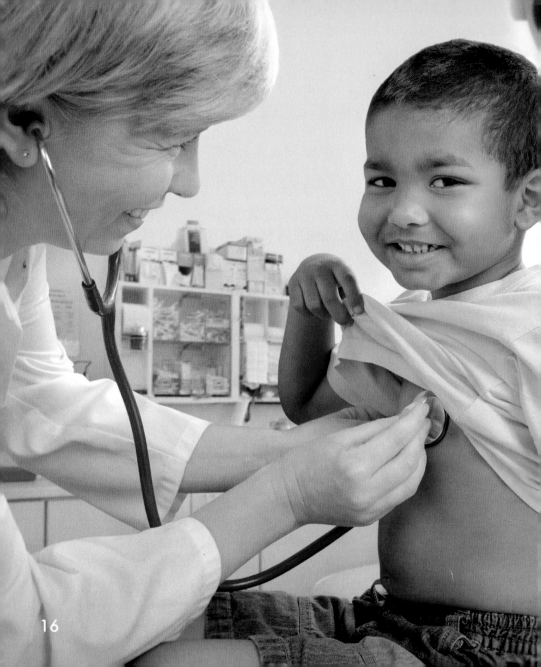

Doctors use tools to gather information. A stethoscope helps them hear heartbeats and breathing. X-rays help them see inside the body.

Where Doctors Work

Doctors usually work in clinics or hospitals. Some doctors run their own offices. Others visit nursing homes or rural areas.

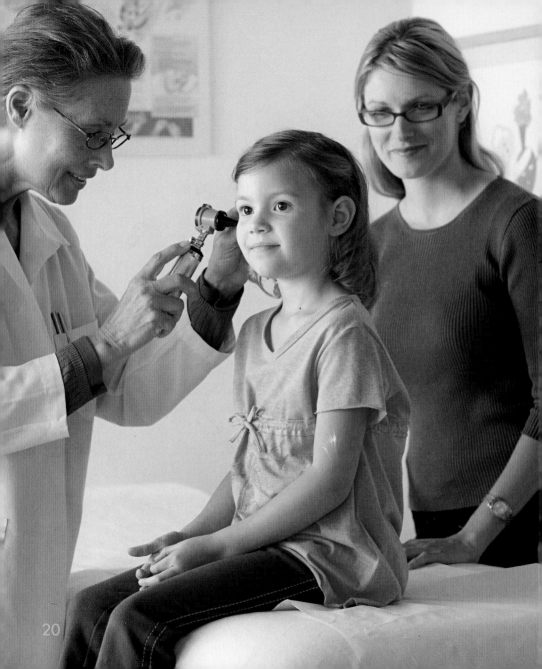

Doctors Help

Doctors are important
to the community.
Everyone gets sick sometimes.
Doctors help people get well
and stay well.

Glossary

checkup—an exam to see if a person is healthy

germ—a very tiny living thing that can cause disease

healthy—fit and well, not sick

hospital—a building where doctors and others work to help sick or hurt people or animals

patient—a person who gets medical care

rural—having to do with the countryside

scrubs—a loose, lightweight uniform worn by workers in clinics and hospitals

stethoscope—a tool used to listen to the heart and lungs

surgery—an operation that involves cutting into the body to remove or fix a part of the body

x-ray—a picture taken of the inside of the body that can show if something is wrong

Read More

Askew, Amanda. *Doctor.* People Who Help Us. Irvine, Calif.: QEB Pub., 2010.

Gorman, Jacqueline Laks. *Doctors.* People in My Community. New York: Gareth Stevens Pub., 2011.

Gregory, Josh. *What Do They Do? Doctors.* Community Connections. Ann Arbor, Mich.: Cherry Lake Pub., 2010.

Internet Sites

FactHound offers a safe, fun way to find Internet sites related to this book. All of the sites on FactHound have been researched by our staff.

Here's all you do:

Visit *www.facthound.com*

Type in this code: 9781620650783

Check out projects, games and lots more at
www.capstonekids.com

Index

Word Count: 176
Grade: 1
Early-Intervention Level: 19

Editorial Credits
Gillia Olson, editor; Gene Bentdahl, designer; Eric Manske, production specialist

Photo Credits
Corbis: JLP/Jose L. Pelaez, 8, Simon Jarratt, 18; Newscom: Tetra Images, 10, 12, Tetra Images/Rob Lewine, 20; Shutterstock: Alexander Raths, 16, AVAVA, 4, Rob Marmion, 14; Super Stock Inc.: Flirt, 6, Science Faction, cover